PETROLEUM REFINERY RELOCATION PROJECTS

5-Phases of Project Management

Rafiq Khadimally, PMP

To order additional copies of this book, contact:
Xlibris
844-714-8691
www.Xlibris.com
Orders@Xlibris.com

ISBN: Softcover   978-1-6641-4524-5
         Hardcover   978-1-6641-4523-8
         EBook   978-1-6641-4657-0

Library of Congress Control Number: 2020924452

Print information available on the last page.

Rev. date: 12/04/2020

Contents

This Book is Dedicated to my Wife
SHEHNAZ
Bless Her & My Family

Special Thanks to My Son
Omar Khadimally, BSPE
To meticulously edit the Manuscript

Petroleum Refinery Relocation Projects - 5-Phases of Project Management
Rafiq Khadimally, PMP

I have presented a paper on the topic of Refinery Relocation Projects previously from a similar Lunch-and-Learn event in a recording in my YouTube channel Rafiq Khadimally PMP. *You may view that for a more in-depth explanation of my thoughts on this topic.*

Introduction

If you take a look at it, there are numerous surplus refineries available all around the world. The United States and the European Union are one of the largest sources of foreclosed or recently closed refineries. This presentation is applicable for any kind of a plant, but I have chosen to do a specific case study to educate myself as well as my colleagues. First, I'd like to share a basic background of myself. I have worked in many oil and gas refineries before transitioning to managing offshore projects as project manager and project interface manager. Currently, I am consulting for my own company, Houston Consulting Group LLC (HGC).

Before we start, I'd like to ask you to ponder on the countless steps involved in this refinery relocation project. My role during this relocation is as a client's engineer. I report directly to a client. As mentioned before, there are many available surplus plants currently in the United States. I do have sources of funding for large projects such as big refineries as well. The main thing to remember is that I do not usually pick up old refineries due to the high turnaround workload. Often in those cases, it turns out to be a giant, expensive issue such as changing the plant's equipment and vessels. The condition of the refineries/plants is imperative to understand beforehand. My main purpose is to guide and facilitate the best conversations between the client's engineer and current plant's owner engineer, to ensure that the proper plant is chosen for reallocation and relocation. These keys and tips of my project management can be applied to any kind of plant to ensure best practices during the refinery relocation.

Petroleum Refinery Relocation Project

Five Phases of Project Management

—A Case Study and Presentation on a 100 kbpd Refinery

Note: This is an addition to a series of video presentations. For many years, I have worked as a project entities manager and have presented on Project Management: Concurrent Engineering on Mega Projects. Moreover, I plan to convert these thoughts and experiences into a book, *Petroleum Refinery Relocation Project,* that will hopefully educate anyone who takes the time to read it. This is a joint education that I would love to share with the client's engineer and owner's engineer.

Houston Consulting Group, LLC
Project Interface Management

Refinery, Oil & Gas, Petro-Chem Projects

Petroleum Refinery Relocation Project
"5-Phases of Project Management"

(A case Study & presentation on 100 kbpd Refinery)

By:

Rafiq Khadimally, PMP

Project Consultant

09MAY20

1

1.0 Safety Moment

My safety moment is regarding near misses in the workplace. Let us say your company has recorded around 600 near misses annually. This can include minor incidents such as walking down the stairs of your building without holding the handrail and missing your step. Even though nothing major happened, statistically speaking, small occurrences like this can add up. My goal is to instill a culture of heightened safety and cautiousness in your everyday life. Even if only 1 percent of those 600 near misses turn out to be a serious fall, you are looking at six totally avoidable incidents. Complacency is one of the biggest enemies in our day-to-day activities. So I urge you to stay aware, alert, and play safe. We all have families and friends who care about us and want us to live healthy lives.

Refinery, Oil & Gas, Petro-Chem Projects

1.0 - Safety Moment

© Confidential - Rafiq (Rick) Khadimally, PMP
Disclaimer: Plan-Proposal by Project Management Professional

2

Refinery, Oil & Gas, Petro-Chem Projects

Safety Moment - Report Near Misses -

© Confidential - Rafiq (Rick) Khadimally, PMP
Disclaimer: Plan-Proposal by Project Management Professional

3

2.0 Mission and Vision Statement

Mission Statement

We are dedicated to delivering effective, efficient, and quality projects with integrity and accountability using both the proven and innovative methods, all while conforming to high standards of health, safety, and the environment.

Vision Statement

To make world the place of choice to live, work, and grow.

As a professional, I suggest that everyone formulate their mission and vision statements, so they can connect to them when networking in the industry, making technical presentations, and fostering a positive professional reputation.

Houston Consulting Group, LLC
Project Interface Management

Refinery, Oil & Gas, Petro-Chem Projects

Mission Statement

We are dedicated to delivering
effective, efficient, respectful, quality and conforming to health,
safety & environment; the projects with integrity & accountability
using both the proven and innovative methods

Vision Statement

To make World the place of choice
to live, work and grow

© Confidential - Rafiq (Rick) Khadimally, PMP
Disclaimer: Plan-Proposal by Project Management Professional

5

3.0 What Are We Discussing?

Abstract and Summary
Three Elements:
- Surplus and foreclosed plants
- Refinery, petrochemicals, power, industrial plants, etc.
- Relocation to developing countries

When discussing surplus plants, many times we are talking about unused surplus plants; however, we are also talking about recently foreclosed plants. Obsolescence could be due to technological reasons, operational reasons, or legal or economic decisions. Many times, the refinery will shut down because of noncompliance with the Environmental Protection Agency (EPA). These plants become foreclosed after they do not have the funds needed to upgrade the facility to gain compliance with the EPA.

Surplus plants are the most economical and picture-perfect solutions for developing countries to take advantage of cost and schedule savings. Due to their circumstance, most developing countries cannot afford a brand-new refinery that costs billions of dollars. Instead, a surplus plant at a reduced cost is the best solution for them. Using a consulting firm, a service which I provide through HGC, I can offer project interface management for clients and serve as these developing countries' client engineer.

I prefer talking to clients directly instead of working through several middlemen. It is, I believe, the best way to ensure clear communication and understanding between the client and owner to guarantee the best deal possible for my client. Regarding my clients, I have sources to facilitate project funding as well; however, a client must be financially credible to pay back the loans in a timely manner. Additionally, potential clients should be able to either provide a sovereign guarantee from the government or a bank guarantee from a reputable bank acceptable to the financier.

In terms of relocation, the USA excels in near-perfect project management to clients in selecting suitable plants. An EPCM (Engineering, Procurement, and Construction Management) project manager must be on-site; the use of 3-D laser scanning (match marking), dismantling, transportation, FOB (free on board) on any port, and shipping to port of disembarkation are all included in the relocation process.

In terms of operations, it is imperative to deliver training of the client's operator team and have contractors for local content—many countries require a lot of local content. Often, countries will have a fixed certain percentage for local content. We will send a team of experienced people to arrange transportation from port, and deal with the processes of decrating, reinstallation, startup, operation, any spare parts, any and all original equipment manufacturer (OEM) warranties, etc.

Houston Consulting Group, LLC
Project Interface Management

Refinery, Oil & Gas, Petro-Chem Projects

What is this About?

- General Introduction
- Three (3) keywords (Elements):
  - **Surplus & Foreclosed Plants**
  - Includes Refinery, Petro-Chems, Power, Industrial Plants, etc.
  - Relocation to Developing Countries
- Some Pictorial Illustrations, . . .

Key Message & Abstract:

- Selection of surplus Plants is the key, vintage, un-used surplus, foreclosures, obsolescence, could be technological, operational, legal, economic, or can't afford upgrades, etc.
- Surplus plants are most economical & picture-perfect solutions for Developing Countries to take advantage of cost & schedule-savings.
- HCG offers Project Interface Management to Clients in Developing Countries with a role of "Client's Engineer".

Summary:

- Relocation: USA excels in defect-free Project Management to Clients in selecting suitable Plants, the EPCM (Engineering, Procurement & Construction Management) Project Manager, 3-D Laser Scanning (match-marking), dismantling, transportation, FOB, Shipping to Port of Disembarkation.
- **Operations:** Training of Client's Operator team, Contractor/s for Local Content, arrange transportation from Port, de-crate, re-install, startup, operate, Spares, OEM Warranties, etc.

09MAY20

7

11

4.0 What Does a Petroleum Refinery Relocation Project Consist Of?

- Process area – includes crude distillation tower, crude charge pumps/rundown pumps, vessels, splitters, towers/columns

- Heat exchangers, fin-fan coolers, compressors, structures, various units, reformer, vacuum units, coker, etc.

- Control room

- Utilities area includes boilers, separators (API, CPI, PPI), water treatment, desalination units, air compressors, etc.

- Storage/Tank farm area – includes crude oil tanks, crude receiving facility via pipeline or trucks, pig receivers, rundown tanks

- Storage tanks are not relocated – Oftentimes, it's better to construct and build new tanks at the final destination. In some instances, small-sized storage tanks could be relocated, but larger crude oil tanks are not ideal. Experience has shown that it is better to build a new tank farm after relocation too. When purchasing a refinery, you can save a lot of money, but you need to thorough negotiation is needed.

- Petroleum products/Sales tanks, liquefied petroleum gas (LPG) bullets/spheres

- Sales area/Loading arms – includes petroleum products sales, truck loading facilities, loading arms, meter-provers, etc.

- Maintenance workshops – includes piping and mechanical workshops, rotating equipment pumps and compressor shop, E&I and control systems shop, civil workshop

- Fleet of vehicles, cranes, hauling equipment, etc.

Houston Consulting Group, LLC
Project Interface Management

Refinery, Oil & Gas, Petro-Chem Projects

A typical Petroleum Refinery consists of, . . .

Process Area:
- Includes Crude Distillation Tower, Crude Charge Pumps / Rundown Pumps, Vessels, Splitters, Towers / Columns,
- Heat Exchangers, Fin-Fan Coolers, Compressors, Structures, Various Units, Reformer, Vacuum Units, Coker, etc.
- Control Room
- Utilities Area include Boilers, Separators (API, CPI, PPI), Water Treatment, Desal Units, Air Compressors, etc.

Storage / Tankfarm Area:
- Includes Crude Oil Tanks, Crude Receiving Facility via Pipeline or Trucks, Pig Receivers, Rundown Tanks,
- Petroleum Products / Sales Tanks, LPG Bullets / Spheres.

9

What Needs to Be Relocated – Project Manager Helps Aid Decision Process

- All process equipment are relocated; large storage tanks are *not* relocated.

- The project manager reviews pros and cons of facility's assets to create a list of the relocated equipment. This may include small tanks, spheres, bullets, etc.

- Plant control system and instruments are upgraded – This will ensure that all instruments will be up to the latest standards to operate the facility safely and efficiently. A source of catastrophic failure for a relocated refinery could be due to faulty and old control system equipment. Avoid this by installing new control systems and conducting a thorough Hazard Operability Analysis.

Houston Consulting Group, LLC
Project Interface Management

Refinery, Oil & Gas, Petro-Chem Projects

A typical Petroleum Refinery consists of, . . . Contd/-

Sales Area / Loading Arms:
- Petroleum products sales, Truck Loading Facilities,
- Loading Arms, Meter-Provers, etc.

Maintenance Workshops:
- Piping-Mech workshop, Rotating Equipment Pumps & Compressors shop, E&I/CS shop, Civil Workshop,
- Fleet of Vehicles, Cranes, Hauling Equipment, etc.

What needs to be relocated – Decision is made, . . :
- All process equipment is relocated, large storage tanks are NOT,
- PM reviews pros & cons to decide what will relocated, small Tanks, Spheres & Bullets, etc., List of relocated equipment
    - Plant Control System & Instruments are upgraded.

09MAY20

10

5.0 Organization Chart

While serving as a consultant for the client through HGC, I will interview the EPCM project manager (PM). There will also be an Engineering Manager, with my leads on one side and contractor(s) on the other side. I have mentioned before that my position is either the owner's engineer or the client's engineer. In this example, I am the owner's engineer. The client is in talks with EPCM PM and me as they search for a surplus refinery. As the owner's engineer, I will be advising the client during the negotiation phase and helping them decide which refinery is best for relocation based on certain analyses such as the equipment condition, when the refinery was first built, how technologically advanced it is, and plant condition. I also help answer other questions, which may include why the plant was closed, which upgrades have already been performed, and what upgrades remain based on the last turnaround of the refinery before it closed.

All known facility documents will be relocated with the plant. This ensures proper reassembly of the plant at its destination. Project interface management occurs between the client and the EPCM PM. Moreover, the EPCM PM has many direct report engineers that work very closely with the PM to ensure project success. I will touch base with each engineer very shortly. The people underneath the engineers are usually available in the developing countries to help construct and rebuild the plant.

The first of many direct reports to the EPCM PM include the Engineering Manager. They are responsible for QAQC or quality assurance and quality control. We have an HSE lead, to maintain compliance of health, safety, and the environment standards. Additionally, we have a Controls/Procurement Lead. The Construction Manager will most likely be an expat position from either the USA or England, for example, but local construction foremen are already available. A Completion Lead will also be present, along with an Operations Manager, who is preferably the same person who has operated the plant for many years prior to the plant's shutdown and will need to be relocated as well. I will always recommend to my client to employ the original plant's operations and maintenance managers as they are the most experienced people for the jobs and can operate the refinery after relocation. Again, HGC is responsible for choosing the most suitable EPCM PM. I will inform the client after making my technical bid evaluation and will negotiate the EPCM's contract along with all other contracts per the client's engineer or owner's engineer responsibility. Prior to plant dismantling, the three-dimensional scanning process will need to be conducted. After getting in touch with the EPCM PM, the existing refinery will be matched marked in 3D. After this step, they will proceed with dismantling and will transport it and install the plant in the new location using an updated control system.

Based on my experience, I would like to stress how important it is to upgrade the refinery's control systems and instruments to the latest standard. The control system is the brain center of any plant, and it needs to be new to avoid technical miscommunications which can result in catastrophic failure. Often, the client can negotiate to get all the plant's equipment and get it at a very competitive price. However, I am addressing the clients wanting to relocate the plant to a developing country. I will facilitate the negotiation process, but the client is the main party to negotiate the terms of the surplus refinery. I will help guide you through other concerns and offer my best analysis to ensure you get a fair price for the refinery. Getting a great deal in this step is imperative, as you still need to fund the relocation process and a new control system. The instrumentation, again, will be renewed completely. In contrast, your equipment will be used or surplus. The new instrumentation will allow the refinery to run like new under the right conditions. You may buy a surplus refinery, but installation will be completed using all techniques of project management that I have alluded to, like a new refinery would undergo. This ensures the safety of all equipment, personnel, and the environment.

Additionally, a hazard operation analysis must be conducted prior to operation of the refinery. Without that, you will never go into operations. The steps I am sharing here are a general overview; clients need to discuss with yours truly to understand the full scope of the project scope using these steps. I will gladly serve as the owner's or client's engineer and will help guide you and advise you all the way from A-Z, as I weave through high-level project interface management.

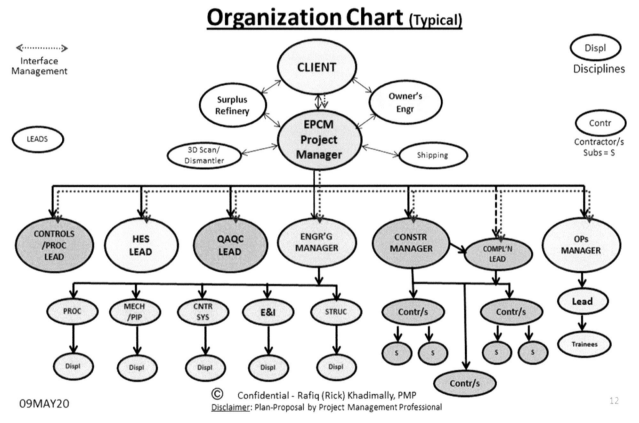

Refinery, Oil & Gas, Petro-Chem Projects

Organization Chart (Typical)

09MAY20

12

6.0 Petroleum Refinery Relocation

On the left-hand side, we have a refinery in the USA. Currently, I am in Houston, Texas, USA. Let us say a client is interested in an onshore refinery. Its origin is the USA and has refinery on-site. We will proceed with 3D laser scanning (match marking), dismantling, creating and transportation FOB (free on board) to the port of embarkation. Refer to letter E, next to the blue star. Relocation will include shipping via oceanic transportation, and we must add costs for insurance and freight. Anytime you have FOB, you have insurance and CIF (Cost of Insurance and Freight).

On the other side, we have the developing country as the refinery's destination. I am going to show this with the letter D on the slide as the port of disembarkation. The refinery will ship CIF at port of disembarkation (Letter D – Red Star), but local transportation will be needed to get to the final resting site. After that, we will be decreating, reinstalling, and conducting the refinery's mechanical completion, systems completion, commissioning and RFSU, startup, and finally operation. We will get two years of spares for operating and two years for capital spares, and OEM warranties. Lastly, all the pumps will need to get extended warranties, and training of operators/maintenance will be necessary.

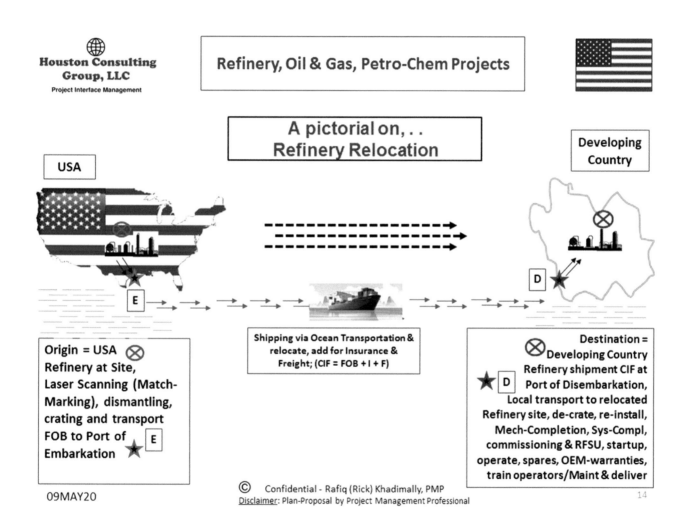

Houston Consulting Group, LLC
Project Interface Management

Refinery, Oil & Gas, Petro-Chem Projects

**A pictorial on, . .
Refinery Relocation**

USA

Developing Country

E

D

**Shipping via Ocean Transportation &
relocate, add for Insurance &
Freight; (CIF = FOB + I + F)**

**Origin = USA ⊗
Refinery at Site,
Laser Scanning (Match-
Marking), dismantling,
crating and transport
FOB to Port of
Embarkation** ★ E

**Destination = ⊗
Developing Country
Refinery shipment CIF at
Port of Disembarkation,
Local transport to relocated
Refinery site, de-crate, re-install,
Mech-Completion, Sys-Compl,
commissioning & RFSU, startup,
operate, spares, OEM-warranties,
train operators/Maint & deliver** ★ D

09MAY20

© Confidential - Rafiq (Rick) Khadimally, PMP
Disclaimer: Plan-Proposal by Project Management Professional

14

7.0 Follow PMBOK - Project Management Body of Knowledge

PMBOK lays out the project life cycle that we follow to successfully execute projects. It starts with the project initiation, planning phase, executing and controlling, and finally closing phase. These steps are very similar to the steps in the project management process. For that, we start with initiation, followed by planning, execution, monitoring and control, and then reiteration. Reiteration is important because if there is an error with an aspect of the project, then you can backtrack to the planning phase and rethink the issue until reaching the closing phase again.

There are five steps in the project management processes which are from PMBOK, and they can be applied to any project, including the relocation of a refinery. No matter the scale of the project, project management professionals all over the world follow PMBOK and its teaching from PMI.org. They would apply the same principles that I am discussing with you today. To summarize my example, I applied PMBOK to relocating a refinery to a developing country. The refinery was foreclosed, the client came by and hired me to help execute the project. I helped and guided them from initiation to closeout. I assist heavily in the decision-making process of who will be the EPCM PM and which company will be leading the EPCM. A project management team will be employed along with local contractors/content who will give the work to very capable and qualified local individuals. However, let it be understood that this relocation can be dangerous due to the fact it is a refinery. Some may assume this relocation is a simple job; however, it is not and should be completed with the utmost care same as you would a new refinery. All the PMBOK steps will be taken and no shortcuts shall be allowed.

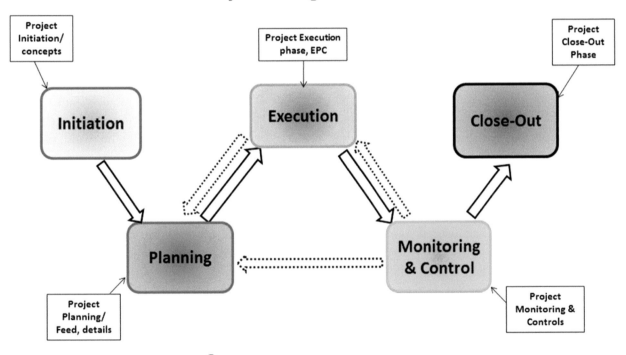

Refinery, Oil & Gas, Petro-Chem Projects

Project Management Processes

Project Initiation/ concepts

Initiation

Project Execution phase, EPC

Execution

Project Close-Out Phase

Close-Out

Planning

Project Planning/ Feed, details

Monitoring & Control

Project Monitoring & Controls

© Confidential - Rafiq (Rick) Khadimally, PMP
Disclaimer: Plan-Proposal by Project Management Professional

17

8.0 - The So-called Petroleum Refinery Triangle

A refinery relocation consisting of three main elements: the refinery's technology, the EPCM contractor who will install it, and operation after reconstructing it. For example, you could have UOP technology in the refinery. I choose this because I have experience with these UOP refineries back when I worked for Saudi Aramco in Jeddah. On the left side, we have shown the original refinery, with its own technology, EPCM, and Ops. The relocated refinery will have a mirror image of the original, and I am helping you understand how that will be achieved.

The Petroleum Refinery Triangle (PRT) involves Technology, EPCM, and an Operations Group. The original refinery operates safely with extensive coordination between the EPCM and the operator of the original refinery. The relocated refinery is an exact replica of the original refinery—helping mimic the original success. Moreover, the relocated refinery must maintain a similar configuration of technology, EPCM, and operator—achieving the trifecta: PRT. For potential clients in the developing world, please pay attention. Never attempt to relocate and operate a refinery in an unsafe and unsustainable manner. I have numerous horrific statistics and stories of relocations that went wrong, which resulted in devastating fires or explosions. This is not as easy as it may seem; however, with my help, we can do conduct this project as safe and efficient as possible. Following these steps outlines the beauty and excellence of project management. If you do not cut corners, rest assured you will enjoy a fully functional, safe, and profitable relocated refinery.

In my professional opinion, I recommend that my potential clients hire the same maintenance and operations managers from the original plant. Their expertise is priceless for the success of the refinery after moving it to its new home. Of course, training of operators and other personnel is necessary, but refinery-specific experienced individuals need to lead the team. We also should remember that the EPCM team will leave the project after the relocation phase. Therefore, it is very important to ensure your plant is in the best hands possible during daily operations.

Houston Consulting Group, LLC

Project Interface Management

Refinery, Oil & Gas, Petro-Chem Projects

Original Refinery

A Refinery operates safely with extensive Coordination within the Technology Group/s, the EPCM & the Operator of the Original Refinery

The "**Petroleum Refinery Triangle**" Involving "**Technology**", "**EPCM**" & "**Operations**"

Relocated Refinery

Similarly for smooth & safe operation of relocated Refinery, they must maintain the same configuration with the Technology Group/s, the EPCM & the Operator of Relocated Refinery

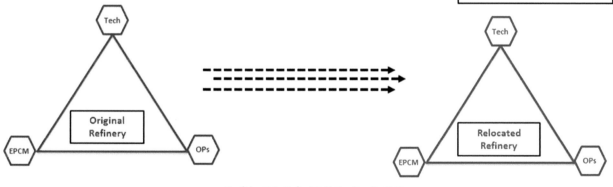

09MAY20

Confidential - Rafiq (Rick) Khadimally, PMP
<u>Disclaimer</u>: Plan-Proposal by Project Management Professional

9.0 Project Development and Execution – The Five Phases

These five phases of project development and execution have been designed by the author, as they have evolved from my many years of experience as a project management professional. Additionally, these phases stem from the steps we have already discussed: Initiation, Planning, Execution, Control and Monitoring, and Closing.

Please feel free to refer to these slides and text anytime throughout your professional career. Moreover, I always welcome emails for any comments/questions. Also, I offer my services and clarifications for any potential clients reading this. The steps I will cover are incredibly important to follow during a project as they help ensure a smooth and safe project execution. However, safety is of the highest priority and always will be. A petroleum relocation project can be very dangerous, and it is not as simple as taking it apart and immediately putting all the pieces together as one found it.

I have worked a total of sixteen years in refineries during my expansive career. Twelve years in one refinery, two years back home in Pakistan Refinery Limited and three years in La Gloria Refinery, located in Tyler, Texas. My expertise is less in operations but focuses more on project management—conducting maintenance upgrades and numerous other projects. Today, we will be discussing a phase-by-phase approach for the five steps.

Project Development & Execution
(Phase-by-Phase Approach)

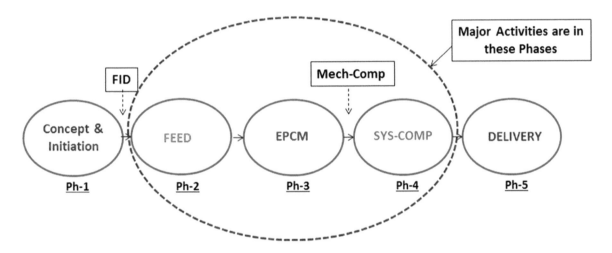

Review – from <u>**Concept & Initiation**</u> **to** <u>**FEED,**</u> to <u>**EPCM & Installation**</u>, and the Mechanical Completion. Then <u>**Systems-Completion**</u> involving Pre-Comm, & Commissioning, RFSU (Ready for Startup), then <u>**Operations**</u> & Startup, Project Delivery.

FID = Final Investment Decision

Mech-Comp = Mechanical Completion

Concurrent engineering is ongoing, saving man-hours and schedule, .

09MAY20

21

First, we start with Concept and Initiation as Phase 1. Phase 2 is FEED or Front-End Engineering and Design. Phase 3 is EPCM or Engineering Procurement Construction Management. Phase 4 is System Completion, which was previously precommissioning and commissioning, but now has been lumped together and referred to as system completion. Lastly, Phase 5 is Delivery.

Most of a project's major activities are in Phases 2-4. After Phase 1, we often complete the FID or Final Investment Decision. This is when you purchase the refinery. Moving forward, when the Concept and Initiation phase is finished, the Order of Magnitude Estimate (OME) of the budget (which is +/- 20-25 percent) has been determined. As the owner's engineer, I guide the client through these phases and through the FID. My client awards the contract, but before that I do an extensive analysis of multiple bids from EPCM contractors. I accredit some of my success to the fact that I always ensure a fair bidding process, after which I chose the best contractor for the project. It may come as a surprise to some, but I often *never* award the job to the lowest bidder. Each interested vendor goes through a prequalification phase when we evaluate them to see which companies will bid to take on the project. In my previous projects, I would conduct a One Bid Explanation meeting. Having all the qualified bidders come into one meeting promotes transparency among the different parties. Each bidder gets a better understanding of their own chance of receiving the contract, which leaves more time for honest negotiation. My team asks a series of questions to each of the contractors and evaluates them fairly. *When potential contractors see this honesty from the client, they will work more honestly for the client.* This partnership is what makes or breaks a project, and my job is to ensure the best project possible. Lastly, I want to mention the importance of choosing reliable, experienced, and safety-conscious contractors.

My client and I will work together in determining the best contractors for the job. This symbiotic relationship will help us both grow and guarantee the best possible outcome. A contractor's merits will be the deciding factor and will help decide which company gets awarded the contact. Moreover, we will investigate the contractors' past experiences and whether they are financially stable. After making a legal and commercial bid evaluation, I will do a cost-benefit analysis to present it to the client. When deciding between the final candidates, it is important never to lowball the contractors for their work. They know the worth of their work and will take offense from this, possibly creating distrust between the parties. Distrust is a precursor to disaster if it festers long enough. This is the reason that I am trying to convince clients in the developing world that you choose reliable contractors to do the job and treat them as if they are your allies. That is the way I treated them, and it brought me only successful projects.

To recap, we start from Concept and Initiation to FEED, then EPCM and Installation, followed by Mechanical completion, Systems Completions which includes precommissioning, commissioning, and ready for startup (RFSU), Operations and Startup, and lastly Project Delivery. Concurrent engineering is ongoing throughout the project and saves man-hours and schedule turnaround. By engineering along the way, we can potentially upgrade the refinery during relocation, which would be the best time to do so. If the client needs new or more equipment, by the time it will be relocated, we could order necessities from another refinery surplus and introduce it into our refinery. This clarifies the need for concurrent engineering, an engineer, and a proper hazard operational analysis. We can also refer to past documents from the original refinery, such as P&IDS, PFDs, pipe corrosion analyses, etc.

By the way, you can view my presentation on Project Turn Around as well. I discuss how to create the scope of a turnaround. For those who may not know what a project turnaround is, it is when you need to do a full maintenance project, for example, on the refinery after you shut it down temporarily. Turnarounds often take three weeks, and I served as the project manager who reports to the turnaround superintendent. As mentioned before, turnarounds is my expertise. Maintenance and upgrades would best be done during the time of relocation, as you do not need to shut down the facility in the near future after starting it up. Mechanical completions (MC) will ensure that new additions to the facility are documented and constructed properly between the EPCM and Systems Completion phases. When MC has been achieved, the refinery will proceed through Systems Completion and commissioning.

Now, let us itemize and recap what we have learned:

1. Concept and Initiation: Review all documentation, plant capacity, process equipment, previous turnaround reports, any planned plant upgrades, potentials to incorporate new technology, finalize bill of quantities, originate OME (Order of Magnitude Estimate), finalize BOD (Basis of Design), Feasibility Report, generate proposal of FID (Final Investment Decision) approval.

Project Development & Execution
(Phase-by-Phase Approach)

Concept & Initiation

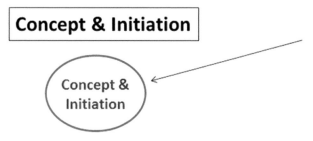

Phase - I

Lets call this phase as, . .

Review all documentation, plant capacity, process, equipment, previous turnaround reports, any planned plant upgrades, potentials to incorporate new technology, finalize bill of quantities, originate OME (Order of Magnitude Estimate), finalize BOD (Basis of Design), Feasibility Report, generate proposal for FID (Final Investment Decision) approval.

Concurrent engineering is ongoing, saving man-hours and schedule, . . .

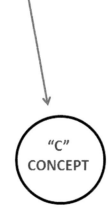

"C"
CONCEPT

09MAY20

22

2. FEED (Front-End Engineering Design): After FID approval, initiate FEED, full and detailed review of all documentation, review crude oil composition, revise HYSIS analysis as needed, revise plant capacity if upgrades occurred, review PFDs, MFDs (P&IDs), equipment lists, line lists, cause and effects matrices. Freeze design manipulation and conduct HAZOP, etc. for EPCM phase.

RIGHT FACING
INSERT IMAGE SLIDE23

Project Development & Execution
(Phase-by-Phase Approach)

FEED – Front End Engineering Design

Phase - 2

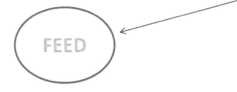

Lets call this phase as, . .

After FID approval, initiate FEED, full & detailed Review all documentation, Review Crude Oil composition, Revise Hysis Analysis as needed, Heat & Material Balance, Revise Process narrative, Revise to cater plant capacity if upgrades, Revise PFD's, MFD's (P&ID's), Equipment List, Line List, Cause & Effects, Freeze design, conduct HAZOP, etc. for EPCM phase

Concurrent engineering is ongoing, saving man-hours and schedule, . . .

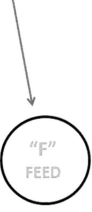

09MAY20

23

3. EPCM (Engineering Procurement Construction Management): After FEED, the EPCM project manager awards all contracts via multiple bidding for detailed engineering, procurement, construction and installation to respective local contractors and supervise via PMT (Project Management Team) the execution of refinery relocation project. Generate AFC (Approve for Construction) drawings, detailed specs, shop drawings, perform QAQC procedures, HES (Health, Environment, and Safety) practices, on construction and installation as laid out in detailed specifications to achieve mechanical completion.

Project Development & Execution
(Phase-by-Phase Approach)

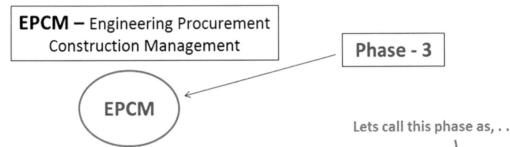

EPCM – Engineering Procurement Construction Management

Phase - 3

EPCM

Lets call this phase as, . .

"E" EPCM

After FEED, the EPCM Project Manager to award all contracts via multiple bidding procedure for detailed engineering, procurement, construction & installation to respective local contractors & supervise via PMT the execution of Refinery relocation project. Generate AFC dwgs, Detailed Specs, shop drawings, perform QAQC procedures, HES practices, on construction & installation as laid down in detailed specifications and achieve "Mechanical Completion".

Concurrent engineering is ongoing, saving man-hours and schedule,

09MAY20

24

4. Systems Completion (Precommissioning and Commissioning): After mechanical completion is achieved, initiate systems completion with precommissioning and commissioning of all systems equipment, control systems, FAT, SAT, etc., to achieve RFSU (Ready for Startup) status and startup as planned with operations group, etc. Operations Group need to be involved from conception, so they are ready to step in when needed. Ensure they are present at weekly and monthly meetings and are copied on every document. Concurrent engineering is ongoing, saving man-hours and schedule.

Houston Consulting Group, LLC
Project Interface Management

Project Development & Execution
(Phase-by-Phase Approach)

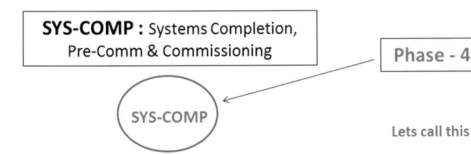

SYS-COMP : Systems Completion, Pre-Comm & Commissioning

Phase - 4

SYS-COMP

Lets call this phase as, . .

After Mechanical Completion is achieved, initiate systems completion with pre-comm & commissioning of all systems equipment, controls systems, FAT, SAT, etc., to achieve RFSU (Ready for Startup) status and startup as planned with Operations Group, etc.

Concurrent engineering is ongoing, saving man-hours and schedule, . . .

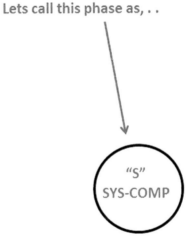

"S"
SYS-COMP

09MAY20

25

5. Delivery (Delivery and Handover): Plant startup with operations group, ongoing training of operators and maintenance teams, workshops for Mechanical Piping, stationery equipment, rotating equipment for pumps and compressors, E&I/control systems, civil works, fleet of vehicles, plant turnaround management (routine, planned, and emergency T/As), utilities, chemicals, operating and capital spares, as-builts, full documentation delivery. Turnaround management is very important as I have mentioned, as there are routine turnarounds, plant turnarounds, and emergency turnarounds.

Project Development & Execution
(Phase-by-Phase Approach)

DELIVERY: Delivery & Handover

Phase - 5

DELIVERY

Lets call this phase as, . .

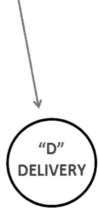

Plant startup with Operations group, ongoing training of Operators & Maintenance teams, workshops for Mech-Piping, Stationary Equipment, Rotating Equipment for Pumps & Compressors, E&I / Controls Systems, Civil works, Fleet of Vehicles, Plant Turnaround Management (Routine, Planned & Emergency T/A's), Utilities, Chemicals, Operating & Capital Spares, As-Builts, full documentation - Delivery.

Concurrent engineering is ongoing, saving man-hours and schedule, .

09MAY20

26

We will apply Value Engineering (VE) based on constructability and Lessons Learned (LL) from previous projects, along with concurrent engineering, to achieve the best project results possible.

Project Development & Execution
(Phase-by-Phase Approach)

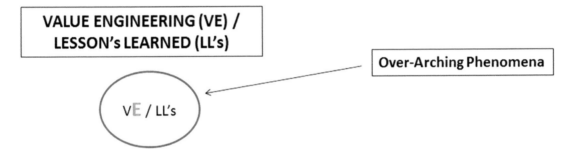

VALUE ENGINEERING (VE) /
LESSON's LEARNED (LL's)

Over-Arching Phenomena

VE / LL's

Apply this over-arching & ongoing phenomena, this is Value Engineering (VE) based on Constructability and Lessons Learned (LL's) from previous projects and captured continuously at every stage of engineering, ... So apply them, . .

Concurrent engineering is ongoing, saving man-hours and schedule, . . .

27

Using the five steps we discussed of Concept and Initiation, FEED, EPCM, System Completions, and Delivery, we are able to create the Olympiad of project management that serves as the basis for a successful project, in our case a petroleum refinery relocation project. I hope you have learned something valuable today, and, please, do not hesitate to reach out to me anytime in the future. Have a great day!

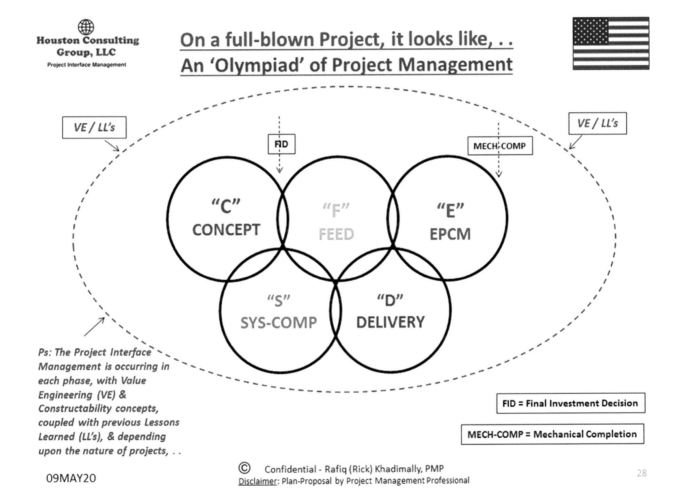

Houston Consulting Group, LLC
Project Interface Management

On a full-blown Project, it looks like, . . An 'Olympiad' of Project Management

VE / LL's

VE / LL's

FID

MECH-COMP

"C" CONCEPT

"F" FEED

"E" EPCM

"S" SYS-COMP

"D" DELIVERY

Ps: The Project Interface Management is occurring in each phase, with Value Engineering (VE) & Constructability concepts, coupled with previous Lessons Learned (LL's), & depending upon the nature of projects, . .

FID = Final Investment Decision

MECH-COMP = Mechanical Completion

09MAY20

© Confidential - Rafiq (Rick) Khadimally, PMP
Disclaimer: Plan-Proposal by Project Management Professional

28

10.0 – About the Presenter

Houston Consulting Group, LLC
Project Interface Management

Refinery, Oil & Gas, Petro-Chem Projects

About, . . .

E: rkhadimally@hcgllcus.com

T: +1. 832-724-6314

www.hcgllcus.com

www.linkedin.com/in/Rafiq-Khadimally-PMP

Rafiq Khadimally, PMP

BSME, MBA – Project Consultant
Houston Consulting Group, LLC

He has managed the crucial aspect of Project Management, performed as Project Engineer on several Oil Refinery upgrades, brownfield major maint-projects, storage tanks & hooked-up during Turnarounds at Jeddah Refinery (Aramco-Petromin), LaGloria Refinery & PRL. Throughout his career of over three decades in Project Management & Interface Management in USA and International he has performed this role as Project Interface Manager on Offshore Jacketed Platforms, TLP, Semi-Submersibles, SPAR, Drilling Rig, Subsea Tieback, Floating LNG (FEED) projects. He worked on Bechtel projects and as Consultant Interface Coordinator on Chevron-Malange offshore project for Angola. He also served as Interface Manager with SBM Offshore, McDermott Engineering (as Project Manager, Topsides) and Wison Offshore. He holds an MBA degree in Global Energy from Bauer College of Business (University of Houston), an Executive Development Project Management program from Rice University, and B.Sc. degree in Mechanical Engineering from University of Engineering & Technology, Lahore where he topped with two medals. He is Project Management Professional certified as PMP, is participative in PMI Chapters and Rice Global E&C Forum events, most recent are PMI-worldwide webinar on 'Interface Management for Oil & Gas mega-Projects' and RGF-presentation on 'Interface Management Energized Concurrent Engineering' respectively. Banking on his vast global experience he is also coaching younger generation as Visiting Professor at JHJ School of Business of Texas Southern University.

09MAY20

30

11.0 Q&A Session

**Houston Consulting
Group, LLC**

Project Interface Management

Refinery, Oil & Gas, Petro-Chem Projects

11.0 - Q & A Session

© Confidential - Rafiq (Rick) Khadimally, PMP
Disclaimer: Plan-Proposal by Project Management Professional

31

Printed in the United States
By Bookmasters